THE ADVENTURES OF TOMMY TRUCKER AND HIS BEST FRIEND JACK

The Load of Ice Cream

Author
Rosalee J Pierce

Editing and Illustrations by Rosalee J Pierce
All road photos taken by Eric R Pierce
Copyright 2013

This book is dedicated to the many animal rescue missions, shelters, shelter workers and foster families as well as the transporters who help make it all happen. Thank you for having a heart.

A special thanks to Paige Nordstrom. Paige created this book cover as well as the Ice Cream Factory illustration.

Jack just finished catching his favorite tennis ball on one bounce when the load alarm went off. BEEP it sounded.

Tommy pushed a few buttons on his computer as Jack spit out his ball on the ground. "Get in the truck boy, we have a load let's see where this one goes!" shouted Tommy.

Jack jumped up on the passenger seat and pushed the button to roll down the window. "It's a load of ice cream and it picks up in Vermont and delivers in Texas next week" said Tommy.

"This will be a long trip boy, we need to stock the truck with some supplies" VAROOM went the big diesel engine and away the two truckers went in search of a store with truck parking.

Down the streets of the city they traveled when they saw something strange on the side of the road. "Look at the dinosaur in the grass! It's a statue of one, I wonder what kind it is?"

Down the road they traveled until they finally found a grocery store that didn't mind big trucks in their parking lot.

"Ok buddy, I'll leave the air conditioner on for you and I'm locking up the truck so behave yourself" warned Tommy.

Tommy walked into the store to get some supplies. He bought some bottled water, bananas, string cheese, purple grapes, paper towels and of course dog food

He packed the truck with the supplies and in no time they were on the road to pick up 40,000 (forty thousand) pounds of the wonderful frozen treat.

Jack sat in the passenger seat watching the view from his window. He pushed the window button to get some fresh air and noticed another little dog in a different truck at a stop light.

The other dog was barking at Jack like crazy to the point where his spit was flying all over the place!

Both drivers just laughed at the little dog then looked at each other as the light turned from red to green. Jack rolled up his window and looked the other way as Tommy drove down the road.

Tommy tuned the radio to a station that did nothing but talk.

Jack got bored and decided to take a little snooze. He climbed onto the bed and pawed at Tommy's favorite pillow.

"Vermont is a beautiful state" said Tommy. The pup wasn't listening; he was on his way to dream-land snoring away on the bed.

Through the countryside down the highway Tommy traveled when later that evening they arrived at the Ice Cream Factory. The Factory was out in the country but still around a few houses where people lived.

Tommy decided he was not going to run his truck at night so he wouldn't disturb people when it came time to sleep. He turned on the little quieter engine that will keep the cab of the truck cool and will not make a bunch of noise.

"Let's take you out for a stretch boy" said Tommy to Jack who already had his leash in his mouth. "There are a bunch of trees back behind the building where you can do some serious sniffing".

Tommy grabbed his big long flash light, soon the sun will be going down and the parking lot will be dark. He then walked with Jack out into a grassy area. They made their way over to the group of trees behind the building. Jack sniffed the grass. *Vermont seems like a beautiful state, the grass smells so fresh* thought Jack.

As the two walked to stretch their legs, Tommy decided to hook Jack's long leash around one of the trees so he could finish some paperwork. "You sit here for a little bit and listen, bark if you see something" instructed Tommy.

Tommy climbed back up into the truck. Jack sat in the grass under a street light as the sun went down.

His eyes and ears were wide open. He listened to the sounds of the night, *what was that?* Thought Jack.

He turned around to watch a raccoon running alongside the edge of the Ice Cream Factory then disappearing into the darkness. *I'm not scared, I'm a big strong dog that's what I am* thought Jack to himself.

He looked up into the trees that lined the road. What he saw were two big yellow eyes looking back at him! HOOT said the creature in the tree. Then he heard it come from another tree, HOOT HOOT then another!

Jack was getting nervous and started to twitch WOOF he barked. Tommy looked up from his computer and climbed out of the truck. "What did you see boy?" Jack looked up into the trees and barked again and again.

"Those my friend, are owls they come out at night looking for some supper. Don't worry, you are way too big for them to eat" laughed Tommy.

"I can see you're nervous, let's call it a night" Tommy said to Jack. He took his leash and walked the pup back over to the truck.

Tommy pulled out the ramp Jack uses to get in and out of the truck and the two settled down for the night.

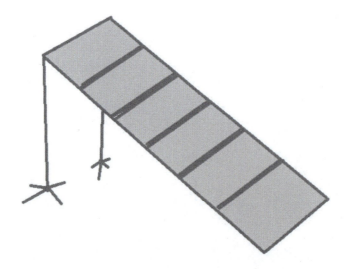

Tommy turned on the TV to see some local news. "Hey look, they're talking about the Owls that have been spotted in this area. I guess there are quite a few of them" said Tommy to Jack.

The pup buried his head in the blanket. He didn't want to hear any more about those darn Owls with the big yellow eyes!

Tommy changed the channel, "let's find out what the weather is going to do tomorrow" said Tommy. Jack had already stolen the good pillow and was trying to get comfy.

"Looks like rain in Ohio, we'll see if we can get that far as it all depends on how long it takes to get loaded".

Tommy brushed his teeth while he told Jack the plan. He washed his face and hands and climbed into bed for a good night's sleep. "I'll take that" as he took back his favorite pillow.

Tommy gave the pup a kiss on his head.

A few hours later, the sun came up and it was time to start the refrigerated unit to cool down the trailer to -20 degrees.

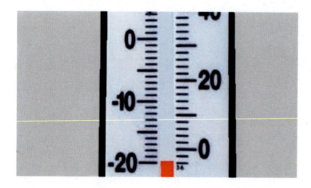

Ice Cream is shipped at a very cold temperature so workers have time to unload it and get it back into the freezers at the grocery stores before it melts.

Tommy pulled on his boots he got from Santa last year and started up the cooling unit on his trailer. He set it for -20 to get ready for all that Ice Cream.

Jack was outside sniffing some tires while he looked up at the trees. He walked slowly as he was still worried those scary Owls would swoop down and carry him away.

"Oh geez would you stop worrying about those Owls. You're way too big for them, They're looking for mice or a fat little squirrel something like that" said Tommy to Jack.

Tommy looked over at the parking lot and noticed some of the Ice Cream Workers had arrived for the day. "It won't be long now boy, we'll be loaded and back on the road soon".

Tommy walked over to see what the cooling unit was doing on the trailer. *It's at -10 now, soon we'll be ready to load up the Ice Cream* thought Tommy.

Later, a man in a white coat and hairnet named Ryan walked out to see what temperature Tommy's trailer was set at.

"It looks good driver, it's at -20 degrees right now. Open your trailer doors and we'll have you loaded in 30 minutes" said Ryan to Tommy.

As soon as Tommy opened his trailer doors, the workers with their forklifts were busy loading one gallon boxes of Ice Cream that were on a skid wrapped in plastic wrap.

One by one 22 skids were loaded. Tommy looked at the paperwork to see the flavors. There was chocolate, chocolate swirl, vanilla and strawberry.

Tommy looked over to see what Jack was doing. The pup just sat in the grass looking up into the trees trying to figure out what an Owl looks like. He saw the eyes but not the body, so he was curious.

Just then, Ryan walked over to Tommy and let Jack sniff the back of his hand. "You're loaded driver, here's your paperwork" Tommy shook Ryan's hand and replied "thank you, have a great day!"

Tommy took Jack's leash and walked him back to the truck. Just then, there was a flutter in the trees, a big old owl flew out of the trees right above Jacks head!

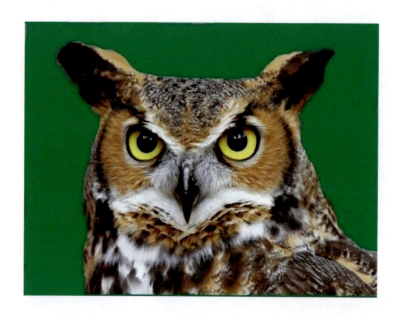

Jack went running back to the truck as fast as he could! Later that afternoon, the two settled in for a nice ride to Texas. Tommy turned on his radio to listen to some music.

As the two traveled away from the Ice Cream Factory, and that goofy old Owl, Jack sighed and nibbled a little of his dog food. He was happy to be away from that place.

Down the country roads traveled Tommy's big rig turn after turn back onto the highway they went. "It feels good to be back on the highway boy, as soon as we find a truck stop, we need to get some fuel"

A few minutes later, he pulled into a Truck Stop to get some fuel not only for the truck, but for the little engine that is keeping all that Ice Cream cold.

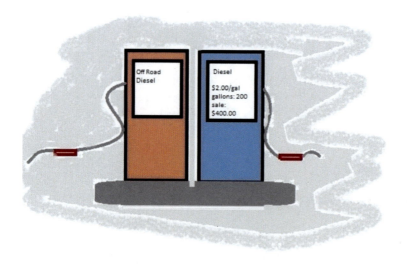

Tommy climbed out of the truck. *We sure don't want to run out of fuel or we'll have a big melted mess of Ice Cream all over the road. Yuk what a sticky situation that would be* thought Tommy.

Tommy finished paying for the fuel and headed back onto the highway.

They traveled for about 300 miles or so when they came upon a traffic jam. "What's going on here?" said Tommy. Jack, had his head out of the window with his ears flapping in the wind.

Tommy turned up the volume on the CB Radio to find out what was going on up ahead.

The chatter on the radio was annoying Jack so he jumped off the passenger seat to get a drink of water. He jumped up on the bed to chew on one of his favorite toys.

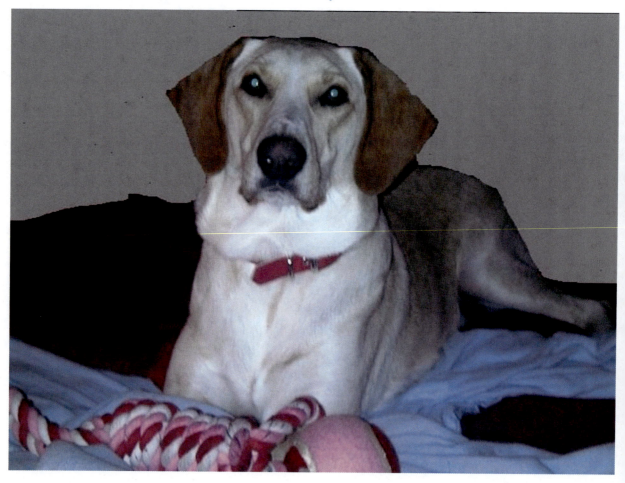

Tommy sighed and set the air brakes. "WHOOSH" they sounded. "looks like we're going to be here for a while"

He then stepped in back to open the fridge for a snack. *What do we have that's good? A peanut butter and jelly sandwich? Nope. A handful of grapes? Maybe. Ah ha here's what I want string cheese* thought Tommy.

As soon as that bag of string cheese was pulled out of the fridge, Jack was drooling all over the floor. "Hold on a second you mooching pooch I'll get you a piece" said Tommy. Jack gobbled up that piece of string cheese in two seconds flat.

Traffic was starting to move again so Tommy took the driver's seat once again. The people on the CB Radio were talking about a crash that happened.

It seemed someone was texting on their cellphone not paying attention to the road and crashed into another car.

"People really need to pay attention while driving" said Tommy. The pup just licked Tommy's wrist then jumped down to sniff the carpet for any crumbs of cheese he might find.

Hours later as they made their way down south, the sun was going down and created the most beautiful sunset. It had the colors of pink and orange along with streaks of blue. Jack had his head out of the window with his mouth open.

Tommy wheeled his big rig into a small Truck Stop for the night. "We'll try to find a spot in the back row to park" said Tommy.

As they drove past truck after truck Tommy was getting worried that he would not be able to find a place to park for the night.

Finally, they noticed one was open. "There's one!" shouted Tommy. Jack still had his head hanging out of the window from before, then he caught a whiff of something very smelly.

Jack started to cough then his eyes started to water. "Woowie wouldn't you know it; the only spot left is the one by the pig hauler!" whined Tommy.

"OINK OINK OINK" cried the pigs in the trailer next to them.

Jack coughed again and again then pushed the button to roll up his window. Just then, he looked at Tommy who was wiping his eyes with his handkerchief.

"I know the stink is bad and the pigs are loud but there were no other places to park" said Tommy to Jack. Tommy turned on the air conditioner, closed the curtains then climbed out to check on the Ice Cream.

"Do you really want outside boy? It's really stinky" warned Tommy to Jack. The pup climbed out to stretch his legs. Tommy checked on the temperature of the Ice Cream.

"It's holding steady at -20 degrees and my fuel level is good for another day" said Tommy to Jack, as the pup lifted his leg on the pig hauler's trailer tire. "OINK OINK OINK" the pigs squealed.

Quickly, the two climbed back into the truck to get away from the pigs. Jack stuck his nose into a vent that was blowing cold air and sneezed shortly afterwards. "Don't worry, those pig haulers don't stay long they travel at night. That driver is probably going to leave after he has his supper"

Tommy turned on the TV to drown out the sound of the pigs. He made himself a sandwich and filled Jacks bowl with dog food and gave him some fresh water.

Soon, the driver of the pig hauler climbed into his truck and drove away leaving a big cloud of dust. "He's gone, thank goodness" said Tommy.

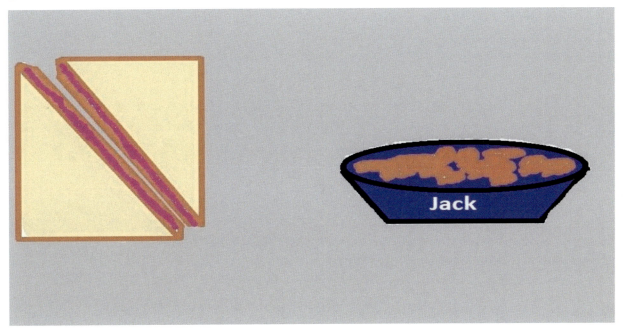

Jack wanted back outside again so Tommy pulled on his boots one more time to go for a longer walk.

It was dark by now with no stars in the sky as the wind was blowing the trees around. Tommy looked up at the dark sky and could smell the rain coming.

Jack jumped back into the truck as the blowing wind was a little scary. Tommy turned on the air conditioner then locked it up tight. "I'll be right back boy, behave" said Tommy to his furry friend.

As Tommy entered the doors to the Truck Stop the wind was blowing harder and it started to rain a little. "What's the word on the weather?" asked Tommy to the cashier at the store. "We're in for a storm sir, there are tornado warnings out for tonight until 11:00 pm replied the cashier *I should look for a safer place to park that's closer to the building* thought Tommy.

"Thanks for the update, stay safe young lady" replied Tommy to the cashier. Tommy filled his thermos with strong black coffee as he knew he wouldn't get much sleep. He headed back to the truck dodging rain drops the best he could. Jack was on the bed panting as he doesn't like storms.

"

I've found a better spot to ride out this storm. We have a heavy load of Ice Cream which will help in the strong winds" said Tommy.

He started the engine "VAROOM" It sounded. Then, he wheeled his big rig over between two other semi-trucks that were parked closer to the Truck Stop. *If it really gets bad, we can run into the building and wait for it to pass* thought Tommy.

He checked the Ice Cream temperature once more, and climbed back into the truck. Leaving the curtains open, he was able to keep an eye on the sky. Tommy stroked his best friend's fur to help him fall asleep.

Sipping his coffee, Tommy didn't sleep much as the wind blew harder and harder. It shook the truck while the rain drops fell like little rocks pounding on the roof.

He watched the skies and tried to snooze a little, but always keeping an eye out for danger. *This is a hard, dangerous job and we have another day to travel but, we will soon be delivering this Ice Cream to the people of Texas* thought Tommy.

Finally, morning came to show the destruction of what the storm had done. Thankfully, no one was hurt and the building was still there. Tommy and Jack walked around to get some fresh air. They walked over branches from the trees that had been blown down during the night.

Today was the day to deliver the Ice Cream. Jack was in the passenger seat wide awake sniffing the fresh air. Tommy sang to the radio as the two were as happy as anyone could be.

The sun was out, the roads were clear of any traffic jams and there was not a cloud in sight. The two traveled down the highway singing and slobbering as that's what they do best.

A few more miles and they would be in Texas. They would deliver the Ice Cream in perfect condition at -20 degrees like they were supposed to.

Tommy stopped at a rest area to let Jack outside. The pup played in the grass with his favorite tennis ball.

Just then, another truck driver drove up with his dog. That dog had a Frisbee in his mouth ready to play. As the two drivers talked, the dogs shared their toys in the grass.

Tommy checked his watch, said goodbye and safe travels to the other driver. Before long, they were back on the road making their way to deliver the Ice Cream.

Tommy wheeled his big rig up to the Guard Shack. He handed the Guard his paperwork. "Take door number 10 Driver" said the Guard. Tommy backed his trailer into door number 10 at the Grocery Warehouse.

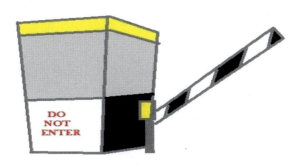

He checked the temperature of the Ice Cream and opened his trailer doors. Tommy was getting unloaded in a matter of minutes, no one wanted the Ice Cream to melt so everyone had to work fast.

Jack was in the passenger seat as usual all pooped out from playing with that other dog. He was watching out of the window as Tommy walked up to shut his trailer doors. The dock worker handed Tommy his paperwork that said the Ice Cream had been delivered in perfect condition and on time.

Tommy started his engine "VAROOOM" it sounded. He gave Jack a kiss on his head and whispered in his ear "I wonder where we'll go next?"

The End

Made in the USA
Middletown, DE
22 September 2022